BIRDS

An RSPB Guide

RSPB

Michael Hodgson

PUFFIN BOOKS

Dear parents,

Birds surround children from the moment they begin to look and explore outside their home. It comes as no surprise that children find birds exciting to watch ... after all, birds are always up to something and many are colourful. This book provides the natural outlet for children's curiosity – so why not join them and learn together about birds?

Bill Oddie

Note for parents

For easy identification, the male of 25 very common British bird species is illustrated and accompanied by a few simple facts. At the bottom of the page is a fuller account, which is for reading aloud to children or for the child with a more advanced reading age. There is a simple diagram to help children identify parts of birds, and at the back is a page of silhouettes to give an idea of size and scale.

Contents

Bird Words

Here is a bird.
Each part of a bird has a name.
Can you read the bird-words?

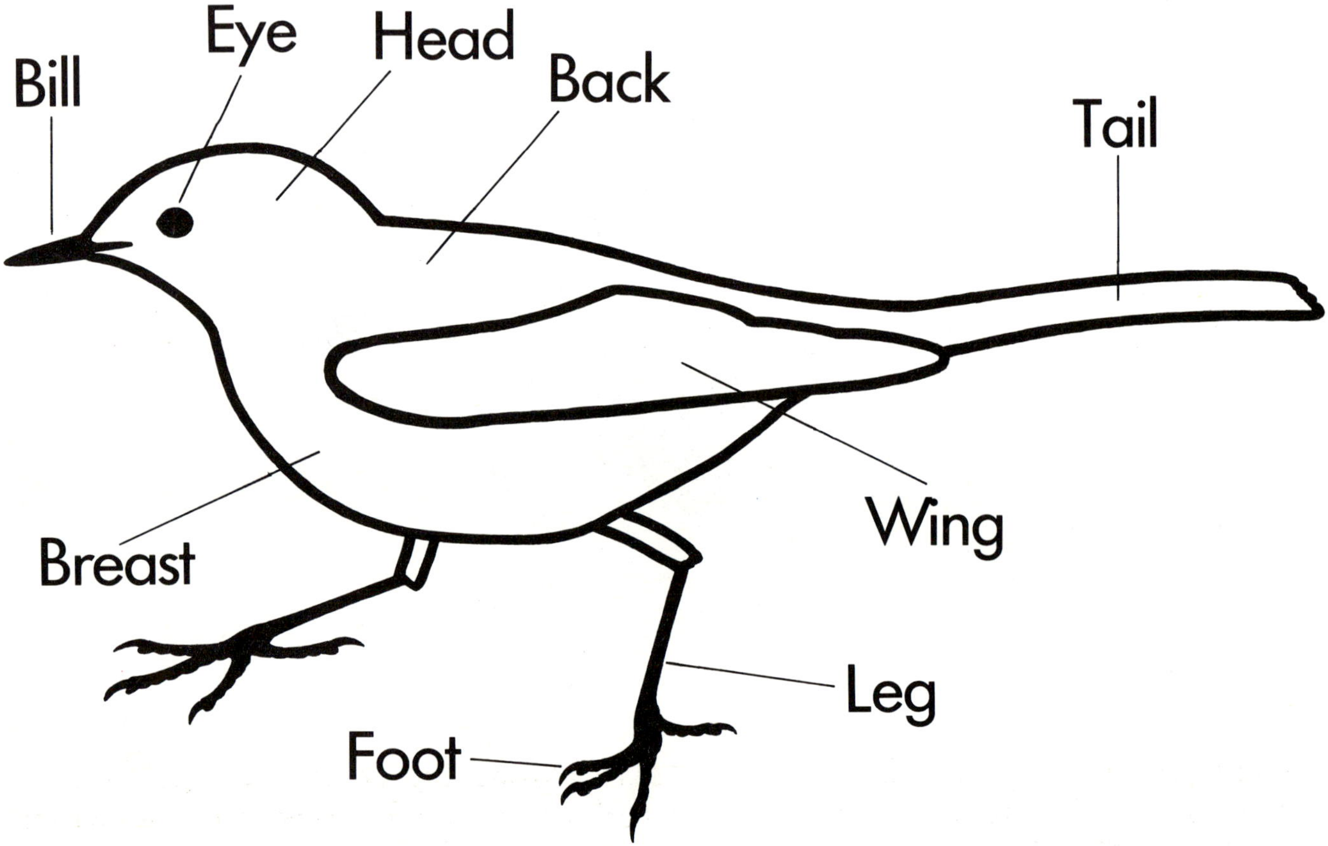

Mute Swan

The swan is big and white.
He has a very long neck.
Have you seen a swan fly?

Mute swans are our largest birds. They are also our heaviest. Mute swans live on rivers and lakes. They have big, webbed feet for swimming. Mute swans put their heads under water to feed. They eat water plants.

Mallard

The mallard is on the water.
The water runs off his feathers.
His feathers on the inside stay dry.
This is why ducks do not sink.

This is the duck you are most likely to see. Mallards spend a lot of time on the water. They have special feathers and feet. The water runs off their feathers, which do not get wet. Their feet are like paddles and help them to swim. Mallards eat mostly plants.

Kestrel

The kestrel can see very well.
He is looking for a mouse.
The kestrel will catch the mouse with his feet.

Kestrels hunt for small animals like mice. They can hover. This means that when they fly, they can stay still in the air, like a helicopter. Kestrels have good eyesight. When they see a mouse, they drop onto it. They grab the mouse with their feet.

Black-headed Gull

The black-headed gull looks for worms to eat.
He pats his feet on the ground.
This makes the worms come up.

This is how black-headed gulls look in summer. In winter, they do not have black heads. They only have a dark spot behind each eye. Look for black-headed gulls on playing fields in winter. The playing fields are full of worms for the gulls to eat.

Town Pigeon

The pigeon is going to fly away.
When he takes off, his wings
clap together.
They make a loud noise.

There have not always been town pigeons. Long ago they only lived on cliffs by the sea. Then they were called rock pigeons.

Then we caught some and tamed them. Now they live in towns with us.

Tawny Owl

The owl can hear very well.
He heard the mouse.
The mouse did not
hear him.

Tawny owls hunt at night. They sit and listen for small animals like mice. Their hearing is very good. Tawny owls fly very quietly. The mice do not hear them coming. The owls catch them with their strong claws. Have you ever heard an owl hoot?

Swift

The swift flies very fast.
He goes high up in the sky.
The swift catches insects
in his mouth.

Swifts spend most of their life in the air. They only stop flying at nesting time. They nest in buildings like churches. Swifts nest with us in the summer and then fly to Africa for the winter.

Swallow

Birds need feathers to fly.
Can you see the
swallow's feathers?
He has to keep them tidy.

All birds have feathers. No other living thing has them. This is what makes birds special. Swallows spend a lot of time flying about. To do this well they need to keep their feathers clean and tidy.

House Martin

The house martin's nest is made of mud.
He sticks the mud to the outside of a building.
It is a very strong nest.

House martins nest on the outside of buildings. Before there were buildings, they nested on cliffs. House martins fill their bills with mud. Bit by bit they build their nest. When the nest is finished, it is strong and safe.

Pied Wagtail

The pied wagtail runs over the ground.
He will stop to pick up an insect.

Do you know how pied wagtails got their name? 'Pied' means black and white, and when they walk about they wag their tails!

Pied wagtails like to run about on the ground. They like to look for food next to water, but do visit dry places too.

Wren

The wren is a very small bird.
He has a very loud song.
His tail is short.

Wrens are very small birds. They creep around under hedges and plants. Wrens are hidden for most of the time. This makes them difficult to see. They need to have a loud song so that other wrens will know where they are. Wrens eat insects.

Dunnock

The dunnock is a little brown bird.
He looks for food on the ground.
You will have to look hard to see him.

Dunnocks are the same size as house sparrows. They are brown like the ground. They creep about like mice. Dunnocks spend a lot of time in flowerbeds. Put some food on the ground for them under your birdtable.

Robin

The robin hops over the ground.
He wants some food.
He picks up an insect.

Robins hop about over the soil. They are looking for insects and grubs. Gardens are good places for them to find food. Their bills are the right shape for picking up small things.

Blackbird

The blackbird has found a worm.
He will pull it out of the ground.
Blackbirds like to eat worms.

Have you seen blackbirds on grass? They run along and then stop. With their heads on one side they watch for worms. When they see a small movement they stab. Their bills can feel for the worms.

Song Thrush

Here is a song thrush.
He finds a big snail to eat.
He bangs it on a stone
to break the shell.

Song thrushes live in gardens, parks and woods. They eat lots of things, but they do like to eat snails. They crack the snail's shell on a special stone. The stone is called an anvil. It has pieces of shell around it.

Coal Tit

The coal tit has come
to the peanuts.
He is hanging onto them.
Can you see the hole
he has pecked?

Coal tits like to find food on trees. Their tiny bills can get at small insects. They can hang on thin branches to look for insects. Coal tits eat peanuts too.

Blue Tit

The blue tit is on the milk bottle.
He has opened the top.
Have you seen blue tits do this?

Blue tits are smaller than great tits. They are clever little birds and are always looking for food. Some blue tits learned how to open milk bottles to get at the cream. Then other blue tits copied them. Now, many blue tits know how to open milk bottle tops!

Great Tit

This great tit has a caterpillar.
He has found it under a leaf.
He will eat it!

There are lots of caterpillars in summer. Great tits know this. They look for them under the leaves of trees. Then they take them to their hungry chicks. Great tits can collect more than 250 caterpillars in a day.

Magpie

The magpie has a long tail.
He is black and white.
He is always looking for food.

Magpies eat all sorts of things. They eat lots of insects. Sometimes they kill small animals. They eat things that are already dead too. You can often see magpies on roadsides. They are looking for dead animals and birds.

Starling

This starling is going to have a bath.
He has to keep his feathers clean.

Starlings like to go about in groups. You will see them walking about on lawns. They stick their bills into the ground to search for insects. Starlings often nest in houses and other buildings.

House Sparrow

Have you seen a house sparrow?
Lots of house sparrows live in towns.
They make their nests in our houses.

You will see house sparrows in most places. The best place to see them is near your home. They are better at living with us than any other bird. House sparrows are always quick to find a new nesting place. A hole in a roof is a very good place for them.

Chaffinch

The chaffinch is having a drink.
Can you see the drops of water
Birds must have water to drink.

Have you seen birds drinking? All birds need water to drink. They bend down and fill their beaks. Then they lift up their heads to swallow. Why don't you put some water out for the birds?

Greenfinch

The greenfinch is on a sunflower.
He has come for the seeds.
His bill is made for eating seeds.

Can you see the greenfinch's bill? His bill is very strong. Greenfinches are birds that eat seeds. Some kinds of seeds are very hard to open. Greenfinches find sunflower seeds easy to open.

Goldfinch

This goldfinch is on the teasel.
He uses his bill to pick
out the seeds.
The goldfinch is very
good at this.

Look for goldfinches in fields, hedges and weedy places. They search for plants with seeds. Their favourite plants are thistles and teasels. Goldfinches sit on the dead flowerheads. They pick out lots of tiny seeds to eat.

Bullfinch

The bullfinch looks up at the berries.
He opens his bill.
Bullfinches eat berries and buds.

Bullfinches are very quiet birds. They are rather shy. Even with their bright colours, they are not easy to see. Look for them feeding in small trees.

Bird Shapes

Wren (9·5 cm)
Coal Tit (11 cm)
Blue Tit (11·5 cm)
Goldfinch (12 cm)
Dunnock (14·5 cm
Robin (14 cm)
Greenfinch (14·5 cm)
Bullfinch (15 cm)
Chaffinch (15 cm)
House Sparrow (14·5 cm)
Great Tit (14 cm)
Swift (16·5 cm)
Swallow (19 cm)
House Martin (12·5 cm)
Pied Wagtail (18 cm)

The Larger Birds

The house sparrow shows how much bigger the other birds are.